Getting Ready To Win: How To Prepare For A Negotiation

What You Need To Do BEFORE A Negotiation Starts In Order To Get The Best Possible Deal

"Practical, proven techniques that will help you to become a better negotiator"

Dr. Jim Anderson

Published by:
Blue Elephant Consulting
Tampa, Florida

Copyright © 2016 by Dr. Jim Anderson

All rights reserved. No part of this book may be reproduced of transmitted in any form or by any means, electronic or mechanical, including photocopying, recording or by any information storage and retrieval system without written permission of the publisher, except for inclusion of brief quotations in a review.

Printed in the United States of America

Library of Congress Control Number: 2016951386

ISBN-13: 978-1537119328

ISBN-10: 153711932X

Warning – Disclaimer

The purpose of this book is to educate and entertain. This book does not promise or guarantee that anyone following the ideas, tips, suggestions, techniques or strategies will be successful. The author, publisher and distributor(s) shall have neither liability nor responsibility to anyone with respect to any loss or damage caused, or alleged to be caused, directly or indirectly by the information contained in this book.

Recent Books By The Author

Product Management

- Product Management Secrets: Techniques For Product Managers To Boost Product Sales And Increase Customer Satisfaction

- Customer Lessons For Product Managers: Techniques For Product Managers To Better Understand What Their Customers Really Want

Public Speaking

- Secrets To Organizing A Speech For Maximum Impact: How to put together a speech that will capture and hold your audience's attention

- How To Become A Better Speaker By Changing How You Speak: Change techniques that will transform a speech into a memorable event

CIO Skills

- Your Success As A CIO Depends On How Well You Communicate: Tips And Techniques For CIOs To Use In Order To Become Better Communicators

- What CIOs Need To Know About Working With Partners: Techniques For CIOs To Use In Order To Be Able To Successfully Work With Partners

IT Manager Skills

- Save Yourself, Save Your Job – How To Manage Your IT Career: Secrets That IT Managers Can Use In Order To Have A Successful Career

- Growing Your CIO Career: How CIOs Can Work With The Entire Company In Order To Be Successful

Negotiating

- Learn How To Package Trades In Your Next Negotiation

- Learn How To Signal In Your Next Negotiation: How To Develop The Skill Of Effective Signaling In A Negotiation In Order To Get The Best Possible Outcome

Miscellaneous

- The Internet-Enabled Successful School District Superintendent: How To Use The Internet To Boost Parental Involvement In Your Schools

- Power Distribution Unit (PDU) Secrets: What Everyone Who Works In A Data Center Needs To Know!

Note: See a complete list of books by Dr. Jim Anderson at the back of this book.

Acknowledgements

Any book like this one is the result of years of real-world work experience. In my over 25 years of working for 7 different firms, I have met countless fantastic people and I've been mentored by some truly exceptional ones. Although I've probably forgotten some of the people who made me the person that I am today, here is my attempt to finally give them the recognition that they so truly deserve:

- Thomas P. Anderson
- Art Puett
- Bobbi Marshall
- Bob Boggs

Dr. Jim Anderson

This book is dedicated to my wife Lori. None of this would have been possible without her love and support.

Thanks for the best 21 years of my life (so far)...!

Table Of Contents

HOW DO YOU PREPARE FOR A NEGOTIATION?...............8

ABOUT THE AUTHOR..10

CHAPTER 1: THE DIFFERENCE BETWEEN SPORTS AND SALES NEGOTIATION: WINNING 14

CHAPTER 2: 3 SECRETS SUCCESSFUL SALES NEGOTIATORS USE TO WIN 17

CHAPTER 3: DEADLY SINS OF SALES NEGOTIATIONS: HOPE AND 3 OTHERS 20

CHAPTER 4: SAD SALES NEGOTIATORS DO A BAD JOB 24

CHAPTER 5: THE POWER OF TIME IN A SALES NEGOTIATION 28

CHAPTER 6: HE WHO WORKS THE HARDEST, WINS THE NEGOTIATION 33

CHAPTER 7: 5 WAYS THE GREAT SALES NEGOTIATORS BUILD SUPER BARGAINING POWER 37

CHAPTER 8: 10 WAYS TO QUICKLY BOOST YOUR POWER IN ANY NEGOTIATION 41

CHAPTER 9: GANG NEGOTIATING: DOES MORE PEOPLE MAKE FOR BETTER DEALS? 45

CHAPTER 10: 3 RULES OF NEGOTIATING POWER THAT YOU NEED TO KNOW 49

CHAPTER 11: 5 QUESTIONS TO FIND OUT IF SOMEONE IS A GOOD NEGOTIATOR..52

CHAPTER 12: 5 SALES NEGOTIATING SKILLS FOR YOU SHOULD BE WORKING ON RIGHT NOW!...55

How Do You Prepare For A Negotiation?

Just about anything that we do requires planning on our part. We need to take the time to understand what we want to accomplish, how we are going to go about doing it, and what kinds of resources we are going to need in order to get it done. It turns out that a negotiation is just like everything else in our lives: if we want to get the deal that we are looking for, then we're going to have to do some preparation.

It turns out that the time that we've spent playing different types of sports has not been wasted. There is a similarity between competing in a sport and conducting a negotiation – in both circumstances we really want to win. In order to get what we want out of a negotiation we need to make sure that we don't just sit around and hope for the best outcome, we need to make it happen.

Our attitude when we go into a negotiation can have a big impact on the deal that we are able to secure. If we go in sad, then we're going to be at a disadvantage. We need to gather as much power to our side as we can and one way to do this is to get time to work for us and not against us. If you work hard at a negotiation, then you'll be rewarded with the type of deal that you've been looking for.

There are a number of different ways to make yourself more powerful in a negotiation. Bringing a team to the table is one way to go about doing this, but there are advantages and disadvantages to doing it. Not all negotiations are done by ourselves. If we choose to bring in a professional negotiator to do our dirty work for us, then we're going to need to know how to find out if they truly know their stuff.

For more information on what it takes to be a great negotiator, check out my blog, The Accidental Negotiator, at:

www.TheAccidentalNegotiator.com

Good luck!

- Dr. Jim Anderson

About The Author

I must confess that I never set out to be a negotiator. When I went to school, I studied Computer Science and thought that I'd get a nice job programming and that would be that. Well, at least part of that plan worked out!

My first job was working for Boeing on their F/A-18 fighter jet program. I spent my days programming fighter jet software in assembly language and I loved it. The U.S. government decided to save some money and went looking for other countries to sell this plane to. This put me into an unfamiliar role: I started to negotiate with foreign military officials and I ended up having to participate in the negotiations for large international deals.

Time moved on and so did I. I found myself working for Siemens, the big German telecommunications company. They were making phone switches and selling them to the seven U.S. phone companies. The problem was that the switches were too complicated. When it came time to negotiate a deal with the customer, the sales teams struggled to create an effective negotiating strategy. I was called in to bridge the world between the product functionality and the business impacts as they related to the negotiations.

I've spent over 25 years working as a negotiator for both big companies and startups. This has given me an opportunity to learn what it takes to both plan and execute negotiations of all sizes. When it comes to negotiations, I've pretty much been there, done that.

I now live in Tampa Florida where I spend my time managing my consulting business, Blue Elephant Consulting, teaching college courses at the University of South Florida, and traveling to work with companies like yours to share the knowledge that I have about how to prepare for and execute successful negotiations.

I'm always available to answer questions and I can be reached at:

Dr. Jim Anderson
Blue Elephant Consulting
Email: jim@BlueElephantConsulting.com
Facebook: http://goo.gl/1TVoK
Web: http://www.BlueElephantConsulting.com/

"Unforgettable communication skills that will set your ideas free..."

Create An Effective Negotiating Team At Your Company!

Dr. Jim Anderson is available to provide training and coaching on the topics that are the most important to people who have to negotiate: how can my team effectively prepare for and execute a successful negotiation that will get us what we both want and need?

Dr. Anderson believes that in order to both learn and remember what he says, audiences need to laugh. Each one of his speeches is full of fun and humor so that what he says "sticks" with everyone.

Dr. Anderson's Negotiating Training Includes:

1. How to plan for a negotiation: what information do you need and where can you find it?

2. What's the best way to explore how a deal can be created during a negotiation?

3. How can you bring a negotiation to a close without giving in to the other side?

Dr. Jim Anderson works with over 100 customers per year. To invite Dr. Anderson to work with you, contact him at:

Phone: 813-418-6970 or
Email: jim@BlueElephantConsulting.com

Speaking. Negotiating. Managing. Marketing.

Chapter 1

The Difference Between Sports And Sales Negotiation: Winning

Chapter 1: The Difference Between Sports And Sales Negotiation: Winning

What does it mean to "win" a sales negotiation? This sure looks like a simple question doesn't it? I think that in our minds, we all know what we think winning looks like – after all, we see it in sports all the time. However, things are **just a bit different** when it comes to sales negotiations...

In sports, winning sometimes is achieved by a **blowout** – the football game that ends up 60 – 0, the no-hitter in baseball, etc. What's interesting is that although these are clear victories for one team, the viewers get bored quickly and turn off the game – why bother if you already know who's going to win. A lot of Superbowl games have been like this.

It turns out that sales good negotiations are a lot more like sports games that are **too close to call** right up until the last moment.

Dr. Chester Karrass goes about **defining a sales negotiation winner** as being someone who *".. understands what his or her objectives are and takes the time to achieve what is possible through the bargaining process."*

The interesting thing here is that "getting the lowest / highest price" is nowhere to be found in this definition – I think that that speaks volumes. During a sports competition, nobody spends any time worrying about **what they can do to make a better deal for the other side**. However, during a sales negotiation, this can be critical because you're going to be dealing with the other side in the future and this negotiation is just the start.

Finally, one of the keys to being a successful sales negotiator is to make sure that the other side ends up **being satisfied** with the final deal that you reach. Unlike sports, it's not over once the deal has been inked. The other side still needs to deliver on their promises and you want them to be happy to do so – not unhappy and looking for ways to cut corners in order to make back some of what they feel that they've lost!

Chapter 2

3 Secrets Successful Sales Negotiators Use To Win

Chapter 2: 3 Secrets Successful Sales Negotiators Use To Win

Ok, so I'll be the first to admit it – I used the forbidden word "win" in the title. In sales negotiations we prefer to not say "win" because it implies that there is also a "loser" and that's not a good thing. How about if we try something like "3 **secrets to always walking away feeling successful**"?

It's All About Patterns

Successful sales negotiators are good at what they do because they know what they are doing. That being said, they also have developed **patterns** for conducting sales negotiations that serve them well. If you want to improve how your sales negotiations turn out, then taking the time to study these patterns will help move you towards your goal.

The 3 Secrets

Control Your Location & Time: Just like most sports teams, the sales negotiator who conducts a negotiation on his / her home turf tends to do better. Negotiating at your base of operations makes life easier – you have better access to information and people and you spend less time searching for things that you need to complete the deal. Additionally, although there is no one perfect time to conduct a sales negotiation, every deal has its own best time. Late on Fridays can often be a powerful time to close a deal quickly!

Understand Your B.A.T.A.N.A?: Before you start any sales negotiation, you need to make sure that you have a good understanding of what your Best Alternative To A Negotiated Agreement (BATANA) is. If the talks break down, what will your next action be? Knowing this in advance gives you more power while you are negotiating.

Start High, Give In Slowly: If you are negotiating to sell something, you need to plan the negotiation in advance. This means setting your price high enough so that you have room to allow the other side to "bring you down". During every negotiation, you will have to make concessions to the other side. Studies have shown that sales negotiators who make their concessions in smaller increments seem to end up doing better.

Next Steps

The art of sales negotiations does not have one magic "sliver bullet" that suddenly transforms an average sales negotiator into a top-notch sales negotiator. Instead, there are a 1,000 **negotiating skills** that provide the scaffolding that we all need in order to climb to the next level in negotiating. Get this right and you'll be well on your way to being able to close better deals and close them quicker.

Chapter 3

Deadly Sins Of Sales Negotiations: Hope And 3 Others

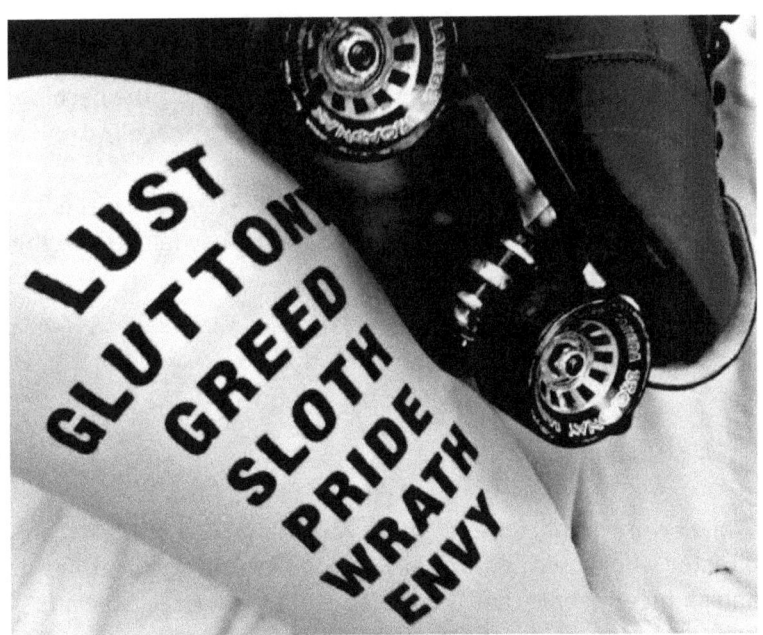

Chapter 3: Deadly Sins Of Sales Negotiations: Hope And 3 Others

We all hear so much about the smooth Donald Trumps of the world that we can fall in to the belief that everyone shows up for a sales negotiation better prepared than we are. Nothing could be further from the truth. In fact, there are **four common sales negotiation mistakes** that even really smart people make all the time. Are you making any of them?

The 4 Deadly Sins Of Sales Negotiations

It turns out that the reason that so many sales negotiations turn out poorly for negotiators is because they enter into the negotiations with the wrong **state of mind**. Instead of preparing for the negotiation, they go in with a "let's hope for the best" type of mindset. How can they possibly hope to do well?

Sales negotiators who have this type of mind set more often than not don't do well during a negotiation. They fall prey to the **four deadly sins** of sales negotiation:

1. No plan
2. Bad agreements
3. Poor reading skills
4. No follow up

While I worked for Siemens, there was a large French-Canadian director who would occasionally explode in strategy meetings and shout at people that "Your Plan Is That You Have No Plan!" In a sales negotiation, this is often the case when people enter into the negotiation without a plan.

Instead of a plan, they have **hope**. Hope that things will go well. That they won't make too many mistakes. That the other side will make mistakes. A sales negotiation is a journey, not a destination. You need to have a **plan** (concessions, demands, questions, schedules, etc.) for how you are going to get to where you want to go.

Agreement Without Clarity

During everyday conversations with friends and coworkers, we all have a tendency to agree to things that we may not have a full understanding of. This is a polite way of keeping the conversation going even when we may not fully grasp what they are saying – we figure that we can pick it up later on.

This same type of behavior during a sales negotiation **can be disastrous**. If you don't take the time to fully understand what you are agreeing to, you may find yourself quickly in a bad situation. Call for a break, take a time out, or ask the other side of the table to better explain something before you agree to it.

Doing A Poor Job Of Reading

Looking the other side in the eye and signing a contract with a big flourish sure can make a strong impression – that you don't have any idea what you are really signing. I learned a long time ago that he who takes the notes, ultimately controls how a meeting turns out. The same goes for sales negotiations – it really doesn't matter what you THINK you've agreed to, it's the words that make it onto the paper that **really matter**. Take the time to read them!

Follow Up, Follow Up, Follow Up!

It's too easy to think that a sales negotiation is over and done with once the last paper has been signed and the handshakes have been exchanged. However, both sides of the table have a responsibility to follow up and make sure that the agreement **is being executed** by both sides. Not only is this a critical part of doing business, it can have a big impact on any future negotiations between the two sides.

Final Thoughts

A long time ago I took a scuba diving class. One of the key lessons that they taught in that class was the simple phrase "Plan your dive, dive your plan." The same thing can be said about sales negotiations: you need to have a **plan** and you need to follow it if you want to have any chance of being successful.

We now know what can happen if you don't have a plan: you'll end up skipping over important steps like agreeing to things that aren't clear, not reading things that you are signing, and not following up after the deal is done. Remembering to plan your negotiations ahead of time and avoiding the 4 deadly sins of sales negotiations will allow you to close better deals and close them quicker.

Chapter 4

Sad Sales Negotiators Do A Bad Job

Chapter 4: Sad Sales Negotiators Do A Bad Job

In the quest to do a better job at negotiating deals, sales negotiators have been known to do some pretty wild things in order to condition themselves to perform at a high level – extreme exercising, exposure to hot / cold temperatures, and even eating some pretty weird things. However, is it possible that they've been overlooking the most important thing – how happy they are?

The Power Of Sad

Dr. Robert Cialdini has spent a lot of time studying how we can persuade others and how they can persuade us. In fact he's written a popular book on the topic titled Influence: Science and Practice in which he talks about what causes us to do things that we may not be giving a lot of thought to.

When it comes to sales negotiations, Dr. Cialdini and his peers have done some interesting studies that should cause all of us to sit up and take notice.

The Big Guess

The social scientist who were doing the research started with the hypothesis that when we get sad, we get motivated to do something to change our current circumstances in order to get out of our sad mood.

They took this thinking one step further. They also guessed that sad buyers would be willing to pay higher prices for a given product and sad sellers would be willing to sell a product for a lower price. Do I have your interest now?

The Experiment

The cool thing about being a social scientist is that you get to test your hypothesis on people, not rats. In this case the scientists had their (human) test subjects divided into two groups. One group watched a sad movie and then wrote a paragraph about how the movie made them feel. The other group watched a movie about fish (!) and then wrote about what they had done that day.

Next, both groups were once again divided into two groups and one group was asked to mark on a piece of paper what price they would sell an item at and the other group was asked to mark on a piece of paper what price they would buy an item at.

What the scientists discovered just might scare you. It turns out that their original guess was right: sad buyers ended up being willing to spend 30% more for an item than emotionally neutral buyers. Likewise, sad sellers were willing to sell an item for 33% less than emotionally neutral sellers. The really spooky part of all of this is that the sad buyers and sellers had no idea that their sadness had affected them so much.

Final Thoughts

Although we often get caught up in preparing for our next sales negotiation, what the social scientists have discovered is that we bring everything else that is going on in our lives to the table with us. On a similar note, the other side of the negotiating table does the exact same thing.

Before you start your next sales negotiation, you need to take a minute or two and evaluate how you are feeling. If there is anything that is bringing you down or making you depressed, then you have got to try to find a way to resolve it or at least make it better before the negotiations start. Learn to do this and it will allow you to close better deals and close them quicker.

Chapter 5

The Power Of Time In A Sales Negotiation

Chapter 5: The Power Of Time In A Sales Negotiation

When I work with clients to improve their negotiating skills, one of the first things that we do is to sit down and review their past experiences with negotiating situations. This generally produces a list of both good and bad experiences. The reason that I take the time to do this is because it shows me where things **have gone wrong in the past** and where my customers need to spend the most time developing their negotiating skills.

Time after time the same weakness shows up in my clients. No matter how confident they may feel about a negotiation or how much research they've done going in, the issue of **available time** seems to trip them up over and over again.

How The Japanese Used Time To Their Advantage

In the early 1980's U.S. businesses "rediscovered" Japan and almost every business wanted to **strike a deal** with a Japanese business in order to get access to high quality, low cost goods. What this meant is that a lot of U.S. business men (and women) got on planes and flew over to Japan to do some sales negotiating.

It quickly became apparent that the Japanese were excellent negotiators. The Americans were coming home with signed business deals that were ok, but **nothing close** to what they had originally been hoping for.

It turns out that the Japanese were not only good negotiators, but they also knew how to read an **airline's flight schedule**. The Japanese would find out when the Americans were scheduled to fly home and they would stall during the negotiations until it got close to the time for the Americans to leave for the airport.

The Americans would be desperate to close a deal and would end up giving too much away just to be able to make their flight. After this had been going on for a while, one American took the time to step back and study how negotiations were going with the Japanese. He **quickly discovered** what they were doing and how they were doing it.

The next time that he was scheduled to negotiate in Japan with the Japanese, he found out when the Japanese that he would be negotiating with were scheduled to take the train home. He went ahead and made **two flight reservations** – one before their train left, and one afterwards. Once the negotiations started, he stalled and the Japanese couldn't figure out why he wasn't getting worried about missing his flight. After he had missed the window to leave the negotiations for his flight, he started to get serious about negotiating. Now it was time for the Japanese to start to get nervous, they were worried about **missing their train back to Tokyo**. In the end, they ended up making too many concessions.

Seven Ideas To Build Your Time Power

One of the fundamental lessons that I include in all of my training sessions with my clients is that time is a crucial element when it comes to **bargaining power**. What it all comes down to is one simple rule: the more time that I have, and the less time that you have, then the more negotiating power I will have.

Now of course, the key to making sure that you have more time during a negotiation is to **take action** to ensure that you have the time that you need. Here are seven ways that you can ensure that you'll have the time that you need:

Leave time to shop around , You may be negotiating with the wrong people sitting on the other side of the table. You may decide to go searching for someone else to do a deal with. If this happens, it's going to take some time and so you're going to need to have enough time to do that search.

Be on time for the meeting , This seems like a silly thing to say, but you'd be amazed at how many people don't do it. If you show up for a negotiation late, then you are going to be running behind during the entire discussion. Being there on time will help you get started in a relaxed way.

Give yourself time to think , Don't let the other side push you into making a decision that might be the wrong decision for you. Instead, call for periodic breaks and give yourself some thinking time in order to reassess where things stand and what your next steps should be.

Avoid marathon talks , Death marches will only end up killing you. No matter how "cool" it might be to tell your boss that you were in negotiations for 8, 10, or 12 hours straight the sad reality is that your performance drops off over time. The one exception to this rule is that if you are pleased with where things currently stand and you'd like to push on to the end in order to wrap things up.

Pick the best time to negotiate , They always say that there is a time for everything and negotiating is no exception to this rule. Are you a morning person or an evening person? Know your preference and schedule your negotiating sessions accordingly.

Leave time for things to go wrong , This one is huge. Things will never go according to your plan. You need to anticipate that things that you could never have counted on will happen, points that you though both sides agreed to before discussions stared will turn out to be significant issues, etc. Leave time to work all of these things out.

Leave enough time to plan , So often my clients will think that planning is something that you only do before you start a negotiation. It turns out that you do it before, but you also do it during the negotiation in order to adjust to events that unfold during the negotiation.

Leave enough time to negotiate with your second choice — If things don't go the way that you want them to with the other side of the table, make sure that you'll still have enough time to negotiate with another partner. There is no worse feeling than knowing that you have to stick with a bad negotiation because you don't have any other alternatives.

Final Thoughts

All too often time starts to cause you to make hurried decisions because you have a real or an imagined **deadline** looming. When that happens, stop, take a deep breath and then ask yourself the following three questions in order to find ways to relieve the pressure of that deadline:

1. What self-imposed or organization-imposed deadlines am I under?

2. Are the deadlines that I'm under real?

3. What deadlines are putting pressure on the other side?

One of the most important points to remember about time and deadlines in a negotiation is that you may not be the only one under pressure, the other side may be **under greater pressure** than you.

If you can learn to make time work for you during your next negotiation, then you will be able to close **better deals** and close them **quicker**.

Chapter 6

He Who Works The Hardest, Wins The Negotiation

Chapter 6: He Who Works The Hardest, Wins The Negotiation

What is the secret for walking away from your next sales negotiation feeling satisfied? We all wish that there was some magic "silver bullet" technique that if we knew what it was we could use it every time we negotiate in order to be able to walk away feeling like our negotiating time was well spent. It turns out that there is such a technique, and it's called **doing your homework**.

The Hard Work Theory

I don't think that I'm going to be causing anyone to fall over in surprise when I tell you that it has been proven time after time that the harder that you work during a negotiation, the better the result that you'll be able to achieve. This is what professional negotiators refer to as **"the hard work theory"**.

An interesting side benefit to the hard work theory is that during the negotiation, the harder that you make the other side of the table work, the greater will be their level of satisfaction with the final outcome. This of course means that they will be that much more likely to **fully honor** their side of the agreement.

It goes without saying that there is another side to the hard work theory. Simply put, **lazy people make poor sales negotiators**. What this means for you is that the next time that you are preparing for a negotiation and are assembling a team, you're going to want to make sure that you have no lazy people on your team!

Using Work Power To Build Negotiating Power

Since the negotiator who works the hardest will generally come out of any negotiation ahead of the other side, this brings up the question of how we can use this **"work power"** to our best advantage. It turns out that there are three principles that can guide us in doing this:

The Least Effort Principle , This principle states that most people would prefer to make their lives as easy as possible. This means that they really don't want to negotiate, they'd rather just say "yes" to an offered deal instead of complicating their lives by having to negotiate for a better deal. What this means for you is that most people won't want to walk away from a sales negotiation once It's started because it would be too much effort to find someone else and restart negotiations.

The Wasted Work Principle , This principle is exactly what it sounds like, nobody likes to waste their time and energy. What this means for you is that once a sales negotiation has been started, the other side wants to see it through to the end. In fact, the longer the negotiation goes on, the more the other side wants the deal to close.

The Easy-Come-Easy-Go Principle , Simply put, nobody really wants anything for free. The other side will not appreciate anything that they get too easily. Instead, you need to make it at least somewhat difficult for the other side to get what they want. Only by doing this will you boost the other side of the table's satisfaction with the final result of the negotiations.

Final Thoughts

The buyer who makes up his or her mind that **"there's always another deal"** if this deal collapses is best able to show some resolve and obtain a better price. However, thankfully, most negotiators are too lazy and subscribe to the three work principles of negotiating: least effort, wasted work, and easy-come-easy-go.

What this means for you is that the more energy and effort that you put into a negotiation, then **the better your odds** of coming out of it with a deal that both sides are happy with.

If you can learn to do your homework better than the other side of the table before your next negotiation, then you will be able to close **better deals** and close them **quicker**.

Chapter 7

5 Ways The Great Sales Negotiators Build Super Bargaining Power

Chapter 7: 5 Ways The Great Sales Negotiators Build Super Bargaining Power

Having some bargaining power when you are involved in a sales negotiation is a good thing. Have **super bargaining power** is much, much better. Most of us do a few things to prepare for a negotiating session, but are we doing enough? The answer in most cases is no. Let me tell you what you can do to fix this…

The following tips for how to gain more power for your side of the table during a negotiation come from the **professional negotiators** who do this for a full time living and who have been doing it for many years. Read on and learn from their experiences.

Prepare To Hear A "Yes"

All too often as sales negotiators we can spend all of our time focused on the deal being negotiated. Since any agreement that we'll be able to reach will be between two people, we need to spend some time focusing on making the other side of the table **comfortable** enough to say "yes".

This has nothing to do with what's being negotiated and has everything to do with the **negotiating environment**: is there plenty of food and drink? Have you taken the time to get to personally know the other side of the table? These things may seem small, but they can play a big role in making the other side more comfortable in saying "yes" to you.

Take Many Notes

If you've ever seen an expert negotiator working, you've seen a pen in their hand and a notepad in front of them. The reason for this is because they know that one of the unspoken secrets to doing a good job of negotiating is **simply remembering what has already been discussed**. Writing everything down will allow you to remember what concessions have been made by both sides and will allow you to move forward instead of just spending time chasing your tail.

Dress Appropriately

One point that is easily overlooked by most negotiators as we prepare for a negotiation session, but not by the great negotiators, is that **how we look** will play a big role in determining how much power the other side will be willing to give us. Normally this means that we should try to dress like the people who are two or three levels higher in our organization than we are. However, if you are trying to convince the other side that your funding is limited, then "dressing down" would send the appropriate message.

Bring A Friend

Being the only person on your side of the table can not only be lonely, it can also be dangerous. Having another set of eyes and ears is invaluable in **collecting information** about how the other side is reacting and how things are going. Negotiations can move so fast at times that there is no way that a single person can stay on top of everything that is going on.

Fortify Yourself With Published Material

This is almost a variation of the "defer to a higher authority" tactic, but if you have **well accepted** external material that you can refer to during the negotiation, then issues that pop up can be quickly resolved (hopefully in your favor).

What All Of This Means For You

The difference between a good negotiator and a great negotiator is not that the great negotiators have access to some **secret powers**. Instead, it comes down to the simple fact that through experience they've learned lots of small details that when taken together serve to strengthen their bargaining position.

What this means for you is that you can move from being a good sales negotiator to being a great sales negotiator simply by taking the time to **learn what these details are**. Once you've mastered them, you'll be that much closer to being unstoppable!

Chapter 8

10 Ways To Quickly Boost Your Power In ANY Negotiation

Chapter 8: 10 Ways To Quickly Boost Your Power In ANY Negotiation

At the end of the day, negotiating is all about power, who has it, who wants it, and what to do with it. You can read every book out there, you can attend every training class offered, you can even do your own field research, but ultimately what you will be trying to find out is how you can **boost your power** when you are in a negotiation.

I've got some great news for you , you don't have to do all of that reading, attend all of those classes, or even do any field research. I've pulled together the **top 10 ways** that you can boost your negotiating power. Without any further ado, here they are:

Set the stage to get a "yes" answer: This one is pretty simple , if you make the negotiating environment a positive one you are more likely to get the other side to agree to your proposals. This means that you need to provide plenty of food and drink and you need to take the time to get to know the other side on a personal level.

Take Many Notes: there is a whole lot of talking going on when you are negotiating and things can get confusing, pretty quickly. The great negotiators are always easy to recognize , they are the ones who are taking lots of notes. This is how they can remember who has made what concessions.

How You Look Matters: when you are negotiating, you need to dress as though you were at least two, maybe three, levels higher in the company than you really are. The way that you look is the way that the other side of the table will treat you.

More Is Better: never enter a negotiation by yourself. Make sure that there is always someone else on your side of the table.

An extra set of ears, eyes, and notes can only help you do better.

Bring Proof: Often during a negotiation you will take a position and the other side will challenge you to change your mind in order to make a deal happen. If you have brought along published rules, regulations, or statistics than you can easily defend your position and the other side will have to leave this issue alone.

Practice, Practice, Practice: Always take the time to practice what you are going to say and how you are going to react the day before the negotiation starts. This is what the pros do.

Keep Your Options Open: don't go into a negotiation thinking that you have to have this deal. Instead, do your homework before the negotiation starts and make sure that you know what other options you have.

It's Not Over Until The MOU Is Signed: when the negotiations have finished, make sure that you are the one who writes up the final agreement , this is the most powerful role in the whole process.

Keep Your Mouth Shut: the more you say, the more ammunition the other side has to use against you. Make sure that you say as little as possible and your power will stay strong.

Always Be Ready To Walk Away: ... and ready to come back to the table. The ability to get up and walk away from the negotiating table is a powerful tool. However, don't be foolish , always come back and see if you can find a way to make more progress.

What All Of This Means For You

Power is a tricky thing in the best of circumstances. During a negotiation, it is even more challenging to deal with. Since it can't be seen or measured, all too often negotiators decide that there is **nothing that they can do about it**, you either have it or you don't.

It turns out that this is not correct, negotiating power is something that the great sales negotiators know **how to grow and cultivate**. There is no one thing that you can do to build up your negotiating power, rather there are a lot of little things that you can do.

Print out this list and bring it along with you the next time that you start a negotiation. Review it the night before the negotiations start and then put it somewhere where you can easily see it during the negotiations. You'll be amazed at just how much power you find that you have after all.

Chapter 9

Gang Negotiating: Does More People Make For Better Deals?

Chapter 9: Gang Negotiating: Does More People Make For Better Deals?

The next time that you are facing a situation that will require a sales negotiation, I'd like to ask you to stop for a moment and consider one important question: **should you go it alone or should you bring others from your side along with you?**

Although you might think that you know the answer to this question, it just might surprise you to find out that you're probably wrong. For you see, this really isn't just one question, but three separate questions that you need to find the answers to...

How Big Should Your Negotiating Team Be?

So there you are, the customer has agreed to meet with you and you know that this is going to be your best opportunity to really roll up your sleeves and **hash out a deal with them**. Stop. Should you go it alone or should you stack the deck and bring more of your team along with you?

It turns out that this question has been fairly extensively studied and the answer is that **you should bring others along**. The reasons; however, are not what you may think that they are.

The studies have shown that when we are going to be the sole negotiator, we generally do a **really lousy job** of preparing to negotiate. Basically we just grab our stuff and go. When we are part of a team that is going to enter into a negotiation, we take more time to coordinate with the rest of the team and we actually do a much better job of preparing for the negotiation.

An additional interesting point is that the more people that you have on your negotiating team, the longer it's going to take you to close a deal with the other side. This makes sense because when there are multiple people on a negotiating team, they will all have to **reach consensus** before a deal can be struck. This often results in a much better deal than a single negotiator could have reached.

What Happens When You Have An Audience?

Sometimes it's all too easy to picture your next sales negotiation as happening just like they like to show on TV: in a big board room with you on one side of the large polished oak table and the other side opposite you. However, often times **reality doesn't look like this**. Instead, you're there, the other side is there, and then there's a peanut gallery of various onlookers. Does this change things?

Interestingly enough, this changes things a lot. All sales negotiators (this means you) have a deep-set **need for approval**. What this means is that we will be highly aware of everyone who is in the room when we are negotiating and we will change our negotiating style simply because they are there.

The biggest impact will be on **how we negotiate**: we'll take a much harder line than we would otherwise because we're showing off. If the other side shows us up or surprises us then we'll take it badly and we'll start to throw up walls to resist the other side at every turn.

Likewise, the other side will react the very same way if they feel that we have caused them to "lose face". This means that you are going to have to be careful how you negotiate when there are others around because your opponent's **behavior will have changed**.

What To Do When You Are Outnumbered

If you show up for a sales negotiation and there are more people on the other side of the table than on your side, you will automatically start to **feel intimidated**. The behavior of the side that has more warm bodies will also change.

Teams of negotiators who have the numerical advantage have been shown to be **more willing to make bigger claims** for what they and their companies will be able to deliver. Confidence can make us say the darndest things.

My recommendation is that you always try to **get a roster** of who will be attending a negotiation session before it starts and then make sure that your team is at least equal in numbers to the other side's. A level playing field always results in a better-balanced deal being struck.

What All Of This Means For You

The right time to determine how many people that you need in order to conduct a sales negotiation is **before the negotiations start**. Your goal should be to make sure that you have the same number of people on your side of the table as the other side has on theirs.

When it comes to making sure that a negotiation is done fairly, I have no problems **leveling the playing field** before the negotiation start. I'll request that anyone who is not a part of the actual negotiations leave the room or I'll ask the other side to kick a few people out in order to balance out the team sizes.

Of course this doesn't work the other way around. If my negotiating team is larger, then I'll be very happy to **keep my mouth shut** and not bring my advantage up. Sometimes silence really is golden.

Chapter 10

3 Rules Of Negotiating Power That You Need To Know

Chapter 10: 3 Rules Of Negotiating Power That You Need To Know

Let your mind drift back to the last sales negotiation that you were involved in. When talk finally got around to negotiating a deal, after all of the PowerPoint slide shows, all of the RFP responses, maybe even the product bake-offs, who had the **upper hand** – you or the other side of the table?

Why Power Matters

The upper hand in any negotiation is held by the side that has the most power. In sales negotiations, **power is a slippery thing**. It's hard to tell how much of it you have and likewise, it's hard to tell how much of it the other side of the table has. Despite all of this, it's a critical part of the process – "he who has the most power in a negotiation will probably end up being MORE satisfied by the outcome."

What all of this means is that you've got to get better at **evaluating the situation**: you've got to know how to find out how much power you have and how much the other side has.

Power Management: How It's Done

Sales people have known for a long time that negotiation is a process of **information discovery**. During this discovery process you learn what your sources of power for this particular negotiation are. That being said, there are three negotiating rules that will help you to learn more about your power during a negotiation:

Rule #1 – You Have More Power: The #1 rule of power management in a sales negotiation is for you to realize that you ALWAYS have more power on your side than you think that you do. Even if you think that you don't have ANY power at the start of a negotiation, then you're wrong – otherwise why would the other side be negotiating with you?

Rule #2 – Power Is Not Real: You need to understand that power is not real. It only exists in your mind and so it is what you think it is. If you think that you are powerful, then you are. If you don't think that you are powerful, then you won't be. Of course this means that you always need to picture yourself as being powerful no matter what the circumstances are. Easy for me to say, hard for you to do.

Rule #3 – Power Flows: The level of power that we start a sales negotiation with is not constant throughout the negotiations. The other side may make verbal blunders and reveal too much, they may make too many concessions, or do other things that will increase our power during the negotiation. Likewise, if we aren't careful we can give away our power during the negotiation.

What This Means For You

These three rules of negotiating power are your ticket to success. At the end of the day, every time that we enter into a negotiation we're hoping that we come out of it feeling **satisfied with what we were able to accomplish** – we didn't give away too much and we got what we needed.

In order to get this type of satisfaction we need to have enough **power on our side** to enable us to get our way on those things that count.

Realizing that negotiating power is a state of mind and that we have control over how much of it we have will allow us to use it to **close better deals and close them quicker.**

Chapter 11

5 Questions To Find Out If Someone Is A Good Negotiator

Chapter 11: 5 Questions To Find Out If Someone Is A Good Negotiator

When you hold up a mirror and look into it, what do you see? Do you see a good negotiator? How could you tell if you were looking at one? This is one of those timeless questions that we are always asking ourselves: **am I a good negotiator?** Well good news, I've got the 5 questions that you need to answer in order to resolve this issue once and for all!

The #1 Characteristic Of A Good Negotiator

Before we dive in and try to ask the questions that need to be asked, let's start off with an answer. The question that we'll be answering, of course, is what is the **most important skill** that a negotiator needs to have?

Lots of people will come up with a wide variety of answers to this question, but in my mind there is really only one answer that rings true: **you've got to be a good networker**. What this means is that you've got to be able to get in contact with the people on your team whose views you'll be bringing to the table. If you know what they want, then you'll be an effective negotiator.

The 5 Questions Every Negotiator Needs To Answer

Ok, you've waited long enough. Here are the **five questions** that you need to ask yourself in order to find out if you are a good negotiator:

Plays Well With Others: Do you have the ability to put issues aside and sit down to work with the other side of the table and search for ideas that will allow both of you to reach an agreement?

Just Like Mr. Spock: Do you believe that others would say that you have a logical way of thinking? If you don't, then there is no way that the other side of the table is going to be able to understand how to create a solution that will appeal to you.

Detail Orientated: Do you take the time to prepare for a negotiation and worry about all of the little details?

Plays With Fire: Can you deal with the disagreement and the confrontation that is a part of every successful negotiation?

Shades of Gray: Can you live with lack of detail during much of the negotiation? Ambiguity is a key part of a negotiation: things don't become clear until the end of the discussions.

What All Of This Means For You

We all want to get better at this skill that we call negotiating. In order to become better, we need to first realize **where we need to develop our skills**.

These five questions should serve as a **great starting point** to help you determine where you need some work. Make sure that you answer them honestly — you won't know where you need to focus your study and training until you have these answers.

Chapter 12

5 Sales Negotiating Skills For You Should Be Working On Right Now!

Chapter 12: 5 Sales Negotiating Skills You Should Be Working On Right Now!

Is it ever too early to talk about planning on what negotiating skills you should working on next? Hopefully not because that's what I'd like to have chat with you about. In order to be a world-class sales negotiator, you have to master literally 100's of different skills from learning how to manage your negotiating power, how to prepare for a negotiation, etc. On top of all that, there are **five areas** that most sales negotiators overlook and yet, they may be the most important negotiating skills that you need to be working on...

The Big Five

You're not going to find this list of negotiating skills written down in a book or learn them in a class. They come from that school that we all eventually end up graduating from called **the school of hard knocks**. Read the list and be thankful that you're learning them now instead of having to realize what you should have known after a negotiation has gone South:

Good Judgment: we would all like to have the ability to make sound decisions. The challenge here is that all too often the only way to develop this skill is by experience and we gain that by making poor judgments. The secret here is to become a careful observer of others: watch the decision that they make and learn from them.

Patience: in our 21st Century world this is an amazingly powerful negotiating skill that all too few of us seem to have enough of. I hate to say it, but it seems that the younger the negotiator, the less of this skill there is. If you can develop this skill, then you'll have the willingness to let any negotiating situation take its time and evolve. Not moving too soon can be a very powerful negotiating tactic.

Persistence: people who don't do a great deal of negotiating often are too willing to give up when they run into resistance. Good sales negotiators realize that opposition from the other side is simply another means of communication and as long as you are talking, there is still hope that an agreement can be reached. Never give up!

Stamina: nobody ever gets into the field of sales negotiation because they think that it's going to be easy. It's not easy. However, the ability to keep at it and put in the hard work that any negotiation requires is what separates the successful negotiators from the unsuccessful ones.

Involvement: at its lowest level, any negotiation is simply a conversation between two people. If you want to have this conversation result in a successful deal, then you're going to have to go the extra mile and connect with the other side of the table on a personal level. It's this kind of involvement that makes people feel comfortable saying "yes" to your proposal.

What All Of This Means For You

Nobody is a perfect negotiator. We all have a lot still to learn. You should always be trying to find out what you don't know so that you'll know where you need to be spending your time **working to become better**.

We've identified five negotiating skill areas that are all too often overlooked by negotiators. We have a bad habit of always looking for the magic **"silver bullet"** skill that will allow us to become more successful in our negotiations. It turns out that no such thing exists.

Rather, there's a whole collection of skills that can provide us with what we need to become better than we are today. Take some time and review this list — **now you know what you need to be working on**.

Hard work does not guarantee success; However, success does not happen without hard work.

- Dr. Jim Anderson

Create An Effective Negotiating Team At Your Company!

Dr. Jim Anderson is available to provide training and coaching on the topics that are the most important to people who have to negotiate: how can my team effectively prepare for and execute a successful negotiation that will get us what we both want and need?

Dr. Anderson believes that in order to both learn and remember what he says, audiences need to laugh. Each one of his speeches is full of fun and humor so that what he says "sticks" with everyone.

Dr. Anderson's Negotiating Training Includes:

1. How to plan for a negotiation: what information do you need and where can you find it?

2. What's the best way to explore how a deal can be created during a negotiation?

3. How can you bring a negotiation to a close without giving in to the other side?

Dr. Jim Anderson works with over 100 customers per year. To invite Dr. Anderson to work with you, contact him at:

Phone: 813-418-6970 or
Email: jim@BlueElephantConsulting.com

Photo Credits:

Cover - Lisa Risager
https://www.flickr.com/photos/risager/

Chapter 1 - AwesomeSA
https://www.flickr.com/photos/awesomesa/

Chapter2 - Wassim LOUMI
https://www.flickr.com/photos/sophotow/

Chapter 3 - Hey Paul Studios
https://www.flickr.com/photos/hey__paul/

Chapter 4 - zeitfaenger.at
https://www.flickr.com/photos/kwarz/

Chapter 5 - Dimitris Kalogeropoylos
https://www.flickr.com/photos/dkalo/

Chapter 6 - Jenni C
https://www.flickr.com/photos/ipdegirl/

Chapter 7 - Ted Duboise
https://www.flickr.com/photos/ted_m8/

Chapter 8 - Donna B. Cooper
https://www.flickr.com/photos/yayaempress/

Chapter 9 - Ari Herzog
https://www.flickr.com/photos/ari-herzog/

Chapter 10 - Miguel Tejada-Flores
https://www.flickr.com/photos/migueltejadaflores/

Chapter 11 - Ryan Van Etten
https://www.flickr.com/photos/ryanvanetten/

Chapter 12 - Rob Albright
https://www.flickr.com/photos/8015956@N04/

Other Books By The Author

Product Management

- How Product Managers Can Learn To Understand Their Customers: Techniques For Product Managers To Better Understand What Their Customers Really Want

- Product Management Secrets: Techniques For Product Managers To Boost Product Sales And Increase Customer Satisfaction

- Product Development Lessons For Product Managers: How Product Managers Can Create Successful Products

- Customer Lessons For Product Managers: Techniques For Product Managers To Better Understand What Their Customers Really Want

- Product Failure Lessons For Product Managers: Examples Of Products That Have Failed For Product Managers To Learn From

- Communication Skills For Product Managers: The Communication Skills That Product Managers Need

To Know How To Use In Order To Have A Successful Product

- How To Have A Successful Product Manager Career: The Things That You Need To Be Doing TODAY In Order To Have A Successful Product Manager Career

- Product Manager Product Success: How to keep your product on track and make it become a success

Public Speaking

- How To Create A Speech That Will Be Remembered

- Secrets To Organizing A Speech For Maximum Impact: How to put together a speech that will capture and hold your audience's attention

- How To Become A Better Speaker By Changing How You Speak: Change techniques that will transform a speech into a memorable event

- How To Give A Great Presentation: Presentation techniques that will transform a speech into a memorable event

- How To Rehearse In Order To Give The Perfect Speech: How to effectively rehearse your next speech to that your message be remembered forever!

- Secrets To Creating The Perfect Speech: How to create a speech that will make your message be remembered forever!

- Secrets To Organizing The Perfect Speech: How to organize the best speech of your life!

- Secrets To Planning The Perfect Speech: How to plan to give the best speech of your life

- How To Show What You Mean During A Presentation: How to use visual techniques to transform a speech into a memorable event

CIO Skills

- Your Success As A CIO Depends On How Well You Communicate: Tips And Techniques For CIOs To Use In Order To Become Better Communicators

- What CIOs Need To Know About Working With Partners: Techniques For CIOs To Use In Order To Be Able To Successfully Work With Partners

- Critical CIO Management Skills: Decision Making Skills That Every CIO Needs To Have In Order To Be Able To Make The Right Choices

- How CIOs Can Make Innovation Happen: Tips And Techniques For CIOs To Use In Order To Make Innovation Happen In Their IT Department

- CIO Communication Skills Secrets: Tips And Techniques For CIOs To Use In Order To Become Better Communicators

- Managing Your CIO Career: Steps That CIOs Have To Take In Order To Have A Long And Successful Career

- CIO Business Skills: How CIOs can work effectively with the rest of the company!

IT Manager Skills

- Save Yourself, Save Your Job – How To Manage Your IT Career: Secrets That IT Managers Can Use In Order To Have A Successful Career

- Growing Your CIO Career: How CIOs Can Work With The Entire Company In Order To Be Successful

- How IT Managers Can Make Innovation Happen: Tips And Techniques For IT Managers To Use In Order To Make Innovation Happen In Their Teams

- Staffing Skills IT Managers Must Have: Tips And Techniques That IT Managers Can Use In Order To Correctly Staff Their Teams

- Secrets Of Effective Leadership For IT Managers: Tips And Techniques That IT Managers Can Use In Order To Develop Leadership Skills

- IT Manager Career Secrets: Tips And Techniques That IT Managers Can Use In Order To Have A Successful Career

- IT Manager Budgeting Skills: How IT Managers Can Request, Manage, Use, And Track Their Funding

- Secrets Of Managing Budgets: What IT Managers Need To Know In Order To Understand How Their Company Uses Money

Negotiating

- Learn How To Signal In Your Next Negotiation: How To Develop The Skill Of Effective Signaling In A Negotiation In Order To Get The Best Possible

Outcome

- Learn The Skill Of Exploring In A Negotiation: How To Develop The Skill Of Exploring What Is Possible In A Negotiation In Order To Reach The Best Possible Deal

- Learn How To Argue In Your Next Negotiation: How To Develop The Skill Of Effective Arguing In A Negotiation In Order To Get The Best Possible Outcome|

- How To Open Your Next Negotiation: How To Start A Negotiation In Order To Get The Best Possible Outcome

- Preparing For Your Next Negotiation: What You Need To Do BEFORE A Negotiation Starts In Order To Get The Best Possible Deal

- Learn How To Package Trades In Your Next Negotiation

- All Good Things Come To An End: How To Close A Negotiation - How To Develop The Skill Of Closing In Order To Get The Best Possible Outcome From A Negotiation

Miscellaneous

- The Internet-Enabled Successful School District Superintendent: How To Use The Internet To Boost Parental Involvement In Your Schools

- Power Distribution Unit (PDU) Secrets: What Everyone Who Works In A Data Center Needs To Know!

- Making The Jump: How To Land Your Dream Job When You Get Out Of College!

- How To Use The Internet To Create Successful Students And Involved Parents

Getting Ready To Win: How To Prepare For A Negotiation

> This book has been written with one goal in mind – to show you how to successfully prepare for your next negotiation. It's not easy being a negotiator and so we're going to show you how to successfully get ready for the negotiation in a way that will get you the deal that you want!
>
> **Let's Make Your Negotiation A Success!**

What You'll Find Inside:

- **HOW DO YOU PLAN A NEGOTIATION?**

- **THE DIFFERENCE BETWEEN SPORTS AND SALES NEGOTIATION: WINNING**

- **3 SECRETS SUCCESSFUL SALES NEGOTIATORS USE TO WIN**

- **DEADLY SINS OF SALES NEGOTIATIONS: HOPE AND 3 OTHERS**

Dr. Jim Anderson brings his 25 years of real-world experience to this book. He's been a negotiator at some of the world's largest firms. He's going to show you what you need to do (and not do!) in order to get the best deal out of your next negotiation!

www.ingramcontent.com/pod-product-compliance
Lightning Source LLC
Chambersburg PA
CBHW060419190526
45169CB00002B/971